ATLANTA

MARY STOUT

WORLD ALMANAC® LIBRARY

Please visit our web site at: www.worldalmanaclibrary.com
For a free color catalog describing World Almanac® Library's list of high-quality books
and multimedia programs, call 1-800-848-2928 (USA) or 1-800 387-3178 (Canada).
World Almanac® Library's fax: (414) 332-3567.

Library of Congress Cataloging-in-Publication Data

Stout, Mary, 1954-
    Atlanta / by Mary Stout.
      p. cm. — (Great cities of the world)
    Includes bibliographical references and index.
    ISBN 0-8368-5042-4 (lib. bdg.)
    ISBN 0-8368-5202-8 (softcover)
    1. Atlanta (Ga.)—Juvenile literature.   I. Title.   II. Series.
F294.A84S76   2005
975.8'231—dc22   2004057144

First published in 2005 by
World Almanac® Library
330 West Olive Street, Suite 100
Milwaukee, WI 53212 USA

Copyright © 2005 by World Almanac® Library.

Produced by Discovery Books
Editors: Valerie Weber and Kathryn Walker
Series designers: Laurie Shock, Keith Williams
Designer and page production: Rob Norridge
Photo researcher: Rachel Tisdale
Diagrams: Rob Norridge
Maps: Stefan Chabluk
World Almanac® Library editorial direction: Mark J. Sachner
World Almanac® Library editor: Gini Holland
World Almanac® Library art direction: Tammy West
World Almanac® Library graphic design: Scott M. Krall
World Almanac® Library production: Jessica Morris

Photo credits: AKG Images: p. 14; Alamy/Jenny Andre: p. 26; Corbis: pp. 8, 10; Corbis/Franz-Marc Frei: p. 39; Corbis/
Mark E. Gibson: p. 21; Corbis/Bob Krist: pp. 23, 24, 25; Getty Images/AllSport/John Gichigi: p. 15; Getty Images/
Jerri Driendi: cover; Getty Images/CNP/Rich Friedman: p. 33; Getty Images/Harry How: p. 16; Getty Images/
Hulton Archive: p. 12; Getty Images/Klaus Lahnstein: p. 4; Getty Images/M. David Leeds/NBAE: p. 27; Getty Images/
Erik S.Lesser: pp. 20, 35, 36; Getty Images/Jamie Squire: p. 37; Getty Images/TimeLife Pictures: Thomas S. England:
p. 29; Getty Images/TimeLife Pictures/Robin Platze/Twin Images: p. 18; Gibson/Mark and Audrey Gibson: pp. 30, 42;
Hutchison/Bernard Regent: p. 22; Image State: p. 34; North Wind Picture Archives: p. 9; Peter Newark/Peter Newark's
American Pictures: p. 13; Photographers Direct/Philip Game: p. 38; Trip/Jeff Greenberg: p. 11; Trip/Adina Tovy: p. 41;
Trip/T. Why: p. 7.

Cover caption: Modern skyscrapers dominate the skyline of downtown Atlanta. The city is the business and transportation center of the southeastern United States.

Printed in Canada

1 2 3 4 5 6 7 8 9 09 08 07 06 05

Contents

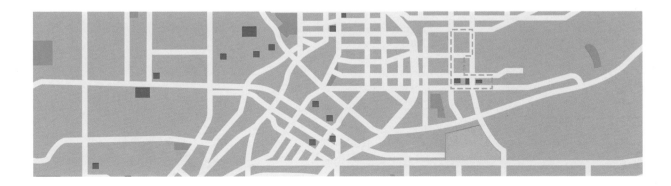

Introduction

Known as the center of business and transportation in the southeastern United States, Atlanta represents the new South, a place where business, beauty, and change combine to form a bustling, lively, modern city. The city's flag and seal feature the phoenix, a mythological bird that comes alive after being burned. Atlanta, too, practically burned down during the American Civil War, only to be rebuilt and prosper as a leading city of the South.

Located in northern Georgia along the west bank of the Chattahoochee River, Atlanta is the capital of and largest city in that state. Spreading throughout the foothills of the Appalachian Mountains, the city lies at 1,000 feet (305 meters) of elevation.

◄ *Atlanta's financial district is the business center for the southeastern United States. More than twelve hundred businesses call metropolitan Atlanta home.*

Its high location keeps it cooler in the summer, while its proximity to the Atlantic Ocean and Gulf of Mexico keep it warmer in the winter. Atlanta's mild climate averages 41° degrees Fahrenheit (5° Celsius) in January and 88° Fahrenheit (31° C) in July. The city receives very little snowfall, about 1.5 inches (4 centimeters) yearly but gets about 50 inches (125 cm) of rain each year. Atlanta faces fierce thunderstorms as well as tornadoes. The city is known for its greenness: grass, trees, plants, and flowers cover the rolling hills of Atlanta.

Andrew Jackson Young, Jr.

An admirer of India's "Mahatma" Gandhi's creed of nonviolent change, Andrew Jackson Young decided to enter the ministry, graduating from Hartford Theological Seminary in 1955. He worked closely with Dr. Martin Luther King Jr. and held a leadership position in his Southern Christian Leadership Conference. In 1972, Young was elected to the U.S. Congress and became the first African American congressman from Georgia in one hundred years, serving three terms. In 1977, President Jimmy Carter appointed him as chief ambassador to the United Nations. From 1982 through 1989, Young was mayor of Atlanta and, after leaving office, cochaired the Atlanta Committee for the Olympic Games. He began his own business, Good Works International, and will be honored with an artwork in a downtown Atlanta park as was announced in 2004.

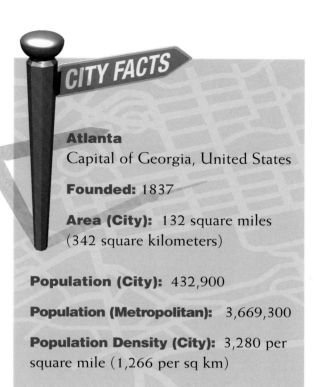

CITY FACTS

Atlanta
Capital of Georgia, United States

Founded: 1837

Area (City): 132 square miles (342 square kilometers)

Population (City): 432,900

Population (Metropolitan): 3,669,300

Population Density (City): 3,280 per square mile (1,266 per sq km)

One of the fastest-growing urban areas in the United States, the city of Atlanta is home to more than 400,000 people; combined with its suburbs, the metropolitan area contains nearly 3.7 million people. Within the city of Atlanta, 62 percent of the residents are African American, and the rest of the city's diverse residents are white, Asian American, or other minorities.

"South of the North, yet north of the South, lies the City of a Hundred Hills, peering out from the shadows of the past into the promise of the future."

—W. E. B. Du Bois on Atlanta in *The Souls of Black Folk,* 1903.

The City of Atlanta

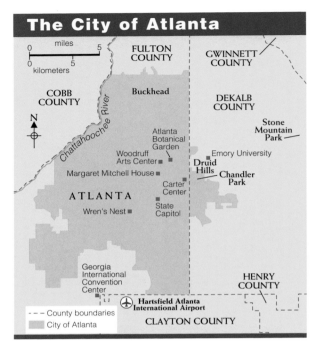

The "Big Peach"

Known as the "Big Peach" (as a counterpart to New York, the "Big Apple"), Atlanta is home to countless neighborhoods. Among the most well known is Buckhead, which is famous for its mansions and also houses the city's financial district. Cabbagetown, by contrast, was home to the city's cotton mill and the blue-collar workers, while Sweet Auburn is the city's historic African American neighborhood. Atlanta's major roadway, Peachtree Street runs north and south through the city's center and is known for its shops and businesses.

Atlanta is the headquarters for more than 430 major U.S. companies, and many top

Atlanta City Center

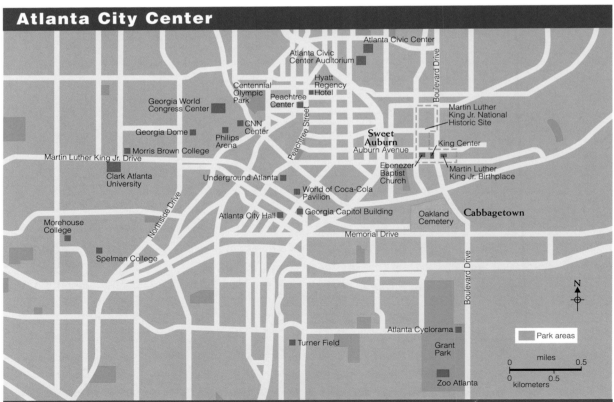

Georgia State Capitol Building

As the state capital, downtown Atlanta is home to the Georgia State Capitol Building (pictured above), which was completed in 1889 to look like the U.S. Capitol in Washington, D.C. Built for just under $1 million, the building features local Georgia materials with the exception of the limestone exterior. Although the controversial exterior limestone was not a Georgia product, using the Indiana limestone allowed the building to be completed under budget. It features a 75-foot (23-m) tall gold dome, using Georgia gold. Housing the governor's office and the state senate and legislature, the building has been the site of many important events.

colleges and universities are also located here. Its status as a major communications and transportation hub as well as the hard work of more than five thousand local volunteers combined to make the International Olympic Committee choose Atlanta as the site of the 1996 Summer Olympic Games.

Atlanta is most proud of its role as a civil rights leader. Reverend Martin Luther King Jr. was born and raised in Atlanta, preached in Atlanta, and helped start the Southern Christian Leadership Conference, which organized many of the civil rights actions, in Atlanta. In 1973, Atlanta also became the first major Southern city to elect an African American mayor, Maynard Jackson.

CHAPTER 1

History of Atlanta

From about 800 to 1500, the Native American Mound Builder civilization flourished in northern Georgia and the Mississippi area. Atlanta itself was originally part of the territory occupied by the Creek (Muscogee) and Cherokee (Keetoowha) Indians and the location of a Creek settlement called "Standing Peachtree."

Although the Spanish had passed through the area, Europeans did not settle around what is now Atlanta until James Oglethorpe, a British prison reformer, was able to band together with twenty other men to form a charter, which King George II then signed. They began a new colony in America where debtors languishing in English prisons could go to start a new life. Named "Georgia" after the king, the new colony, started in 1733, did not allow slavery or alcohol. In 1776, Georgia became the fourth colony to join the newly formed United States of America.

Pressure from neighboring slaveholding colonies caused Georgia to repeal its ban against slavery in 1749, and by 1791, approximately one-third of Georgia's population were slaves. The state's economy was based upon growing cotton, made possible by slave labor. Georgia also became a destination for many poor people and also

◄ *Most of Atlanta stood in ruins following its capture by Union forces in 1864. These buildings stood close by the Chattanooga Railroad and rebel fortifications.*

a haven for those suffering from religious persecution. With the arrival of Jews, Moravians, and Austrian Lutherans, Georgia quickly became the most diverse colony in the Americas. In 1813, a fort and trading post were established at Standing Peachtree on the Chattahoochee River.

As American settlers moved onto Creek land, conflicts arose. A group of Creeks called the "Red Sticks" attacked the settlers, leading to the Creek War of 1813 to 1814. The victorious United States required the Creeks to give up millions of acres of land (including Atlanta) and move to Indian Territory in today's Oklahoma with the Cherokees, Chickasaws, Choctaws, and Seminoles. During the cold winter of 1836 to 1837, the U.S. Army marched the Creeks 800 miles (1,300 kilometers) in the cold without adequate food or clothing in a walk now known as the Trail of Tears.

In 1837, the Western and Atlantic Railroad selected a location near the Standing Peachtree trading post to be the end of its line and established a new town named Terminus there. It was renamed Marthasville in 1843, then a railroad executive renamed it again two years later. It became Atlanta and was chartered as a city in Georgia in 1847.

A Raging Inferno
The state of Georgia joined the Confederate States of America in 1861. Shortly thereafter, the American Civil War (1861–1865) began. Because of its many

Creek (Muscogee) Indians

The original inhabitants of the area now known as Atlanta, Creek Indians (pictured above) and Cherokee Indians lived in houses made of wooden poles and mud with thatched roofs in towns built around a ceremonial plaza. The women farmed corn, beans, and squash, while the men hunted and engaged in war with neighboring tribes. Their most important ceremony was the Green Corn Ceremony, which was held midsummer and celebrated the first harvest.

▲ *This picture, taken in 1864, shows Union troops in a captured Confederate fort near the city of Atlanta.*

"You might as well appeal against the thunder-storm as against these terrible hardships of war. They are inevitable, and the only way the people of Atlanta can hope once more to live in peace and quiet at home, is to stop the war, which can only be done by admitting that it began in error and is perpetuated in pride."

—General William T. Sherman to Atlanta Mayor James Calhoun in a letter dated September 12, 1864.

railroads, Atlanta quickly became the main shipping point for Confederate supplies. Union General William T. Sherman captured the city of Atlanta in September 1864, ordered the inhabitants to leave town, and set fire to the city, destroying more than two-thirds of all buildings.

After the Civil War, troops continued to occupy the city for the next ten years as it rebuilt from the fire. A local newsman, Henry Grady, used his newspaper, the *Atlanta*

Constitution, to urge the citizens to grow crops other than cotton and to begin manufacturing businesses. He began using the term *New South* to refer to a future economy that did not depend on slaves and plantations. By 1867, the railroads were running again, and new textile and other businesses were begun. Atlanta became the economic center of the state, so the Georgia legislature moved there from Milledgeville in 1868; it has been the state capital ever since.

A Difficult New Beginning

Atlanta's roads and railroads were quickly rebuilt after the Civil War, but people's lives were not. Former African slaves were not welcomed into the new life of Atlanta but forced to live lives apart from the rest of the population. Georgia passed segregation laws that separated blacks from whites.

Because they had no training to do anything else, most of the newly freed slaves, approximately 40 percent of the state's population, turned to sharecropping. This agricultural system allowed landowners to lease their land to the sharecroppers, who lived on it and raised crops, giving half of each harvest to the owner. When crops failed, however, sharecroppers went into debt to the landowner and others. Even when crops flourished, sharecroppers rarely made enough money to get out of debt or buy the land they worked.

With their businesses and homes destroyed and lacking cash, most Atlantans found it difficult to begin new businesses after the war. Called carpetbaggers, businessmen from the North came to make a profit throughout the South and started many new businesses in Atlanta.

Cotton, Clothing, and Coca-Cola

By 1880, Atlanta had become Georgia's largest city. In 1881, the city hosted the International Cotton Exposition, which drew 350,000 people and featured cotton mills built for the show. After its close, these mills were converted to a textile mill, which began operation in 1882, and Atlanta became known as a textile center. In 1886, another

▼ *Coca-Cola's long history is traced in the many items on display at Atlanta's World of Coca-Cola Pavilion.*

Atlanta's Race Riot

In 1906, a political campaign for governor of Georgia encouraged hatred between blacks and whites when the candidates spoke in favor of taking away African American's right to vote. In addition, newspapers falsely reported a crime wave by African Americans, which made white citizens fearful and angry. On September 22, 1906, an armed mob of white men roamed the streets of Atlanta looking for African Americans to attack. Many African Americans fought back, and the officially reported result was twelve deaths, mostly African American, and untold injuries on both sides. No one was brought to justice for the deaths.

▲ *In the 1920s, most African Americans in Atlanta lived in African American neighborhoods where the children attended segregated schools.*

key business was born in Atlanta in 1886 when J. S. Pemberton mixed up a new drink in the backyard of his Atlanta drugstore—a drink later known as Coca-Cola.

Delighted with the results of their first exposition, Atlanta hosted two more in 1887 and 1895. At the 1895 Cotton States and International Exposition in Atlanta, civil rights spokesman Booker T. Washington made a famous speech urging his fellow African Americans to seek financial security before striving for equality. His suggestion, called the "Atlanta Compromise," could not stop the racial conflict that had become a daily part of life.

Fire struck again in Atlanta on May 21, 1917, and the northeastern section of the city was once more in flames. More than 300 acres (120 hectares) and nearly two thousand buildings were lost to fire. Luckily, no one died, and Atlanta was again rebuilt.

In 1936, the first federally funded low-income housing project opened in Atlanta. The housing project, built with $3 million in federal funds, cleared a slum area and replaced it with affordable low-rent housing, providing many poor whites and African Americans with modern homes containing running water and indoor plumbing. The same year, local author Margaret Mitchell's *Gone with the Wind* became a bestseller. Three years later, the world movie premiere of this romance of Atlanta during the Civil War was held at Atlanta's Loew's Grand Theater with Clark Gable and other Hollywood legends attending. Unlike the destruction of the Civil War, World War II (1939–1945) brought new military industries to Atlanta. The city soon became a center for airline as well as rail transportation.

Civil Rights Movement and City Growth

During the 1960s, Atlanta played a lead role in the American Civil Rights Movement. Dr. Martin Luther King Jr. helped found the Southern Christian Leadership Conference in Atlanta in 1957 and made many speeches favoring school integration and equality among the races. Avoiding many mistakes of

Gone with the Wind

Published in 1936, Margaret Mitchell's first novel, Gone with the Wind, was not realistic, and the author admitted that she wrote it for her own entertainment while recovering from a broken ankle. Starring Clark Gable and Vivien Leigh, the movie portrayed the South during the Civil War, featuring the burning of Atlanta, and won ten Academy Awards. Many people think about its version of the South whenever Atlanta is mentioned. The movie poster (pictured above) showed the actors against a background of war-torn Atlanta.

some other schools in the South, Atlanta schools were integrated peacefully.

A period of major growth, the 1960s also saw the completion of the Atlanta-Fulton County Stadium and the beginnings of the Metropolitan Atlanta Rapid Transit Authority (MARTA), a modern light-rail transportation system. Atlantans were proud of their slogan: "The city too busy to hate."

The city's population peaked in 1970 with over 487,000 inhabitants, but over the next two decades, the number of people moving to the suburbs surrounding the city increased. During this time, Atlanta's

Dr. Martin Luther King Jr.

Born in 1929 as the son of the minister of the Ebenezer Baptist Church in Atlanta, Dr. Martin Luther King Jr. (pictured left), followed in his father's footsteps after graduating from Morehouse College in Atlanta. In 1948, he was ordained as a minister and received a doctorate in philosophy in 1955. With the aim of ending legal segregation of the races in the country, King and other black leaders formed the Southern Christian Leadership Conference. King quickly became a leader for the Civil Rights Movement in the United States. Influenced by Gandhi's philosophy of peaceful protest and direct action, he led sit-ins at "whites only" lunch counters, boycotted segregated buses, and led many peaceful marches, including the famous March on Washington in 1963, where he made his "I Have a Dream" speech. He cried out, "I have a dream that my four little children will one day live in a nation where they will be judged not by the color of their skin but by the content of their character." In 1964, the U.S. Congress passed the Civil Rights Act, and Martin Luther King Jr. won the Nobel Peace Prize. He was assassinated in 1968.

▲ A crowd of 83,000 people filled Atlanta's Olympic Stadium to watch the spectacular opening ceremony of the 1996 Summer Olympic Games.

businesses also grew and expanded. Peachtree Center was built, offering easy pedestrian access to a huge variety of stores, restaurants, and businesses. Ted Turner turned the Omni International Complex into the CNN Center, the Cable News Network's office building, in 1986. A newly remodeled Underground Atlanta, another entertainment complex, reopened in 1989, and in 1996, Atlanta hosted the Summer Olympic Games.

As the twenty-first century began, Atlanta continued to develop into an attractive place to live and work. Its success is evident; Atlanta in 2004 was hailed as the best place in the nation to locate a business and is one of the top cities for arts and culture. Today's Atlanta has not lost the unique qualities owed to its Southern and African American history.

A Peachy Place

Atlanta's original Creek name, "Standing Peachtree," has continued to be honored by later residents, as they enthusiastically adopted the peach as a symbol of their city. Although not native to the area, peach trees have been planted and flourish, and hundreds of streets and businesses have been named after the peach. Peach cobbler represents Atlanta the same way apple pie has come to mean America.

CHAPTER 2

People of Atlanta

Although the actual city lies in two counties, the Atlanta region includes twenty-eight different counties according to the U.S. census. The city of Atlanta is home to nearly a half million people, including 61 percent African Americans, 33 percent whites (including Hispanics), and 2 percent Asians. The fastest-growing ethnic group is Hispanic. While they represented only 4.5 percent of the total population in 2002, that number represents an increase of nearly ten times the number of Hispanics living in Atlanta in 1980. Hispanics, especially those who originally came from Mexico, continue to flock to the city. Atlanta's diversity is still growing: From 1990 to 2000, its foreign-born population increased by more than two and one-half times.

The average household income in Atlanta is fairly high compared to both national averages and the rest of Georgia and will probably increase as more women continue to enter the workforce. Many families live in suburban communities surrounding Atlanta, and the parents travel to the city each day to work. Many Atlantans are concerned about the rising cost of living in their city, even though it is not high compared to other large U.S. cities.

◀ *Thousands of Atlantans lined the streets to cheer the Olympic Flame as it was carried through the city during the 2004 Olympic Torch Relay.*

European, Latin, and Asian Americans, and Others

The first Europeans to settle in the colony of Georgia were mostly English, German, and Scottish. Their sons and daughters formed the white society that built early Atlanta and became railroad owners, storekeepers, and businesspeople. During the Civil Rights Movement, change came hard, but eventually Atlanta became an integrated society. The city itself, however, lost many white residents to "white flight" when they moved to the suburbs in the 1960s, 1970s, and 1980s. White residents are now moving back into the downtown Atlanta area in a new trend that began in the 1990s and continues today.

Since the first German Jews arrived in the railroad town of Terminus in 1845, Atlanta has always had a close-knit Jewish community. The Jews have built a strong tradition of charity and support of the arts and culture of the city. Throughout Atlanta's history, however, hate groups have occasionally targeted the Jewish community. In 1915, for example, an accused murderer, Leo Frank, a Jew, was lynched, and a temple was bombed in 1958 because of its rabbi's support of the Civil Rights Movement.

African Americans: From Slavery to Segregation

Originally brought to Georgia as slaves, African Americans became sharecroppers and laborers after the Civil War. The

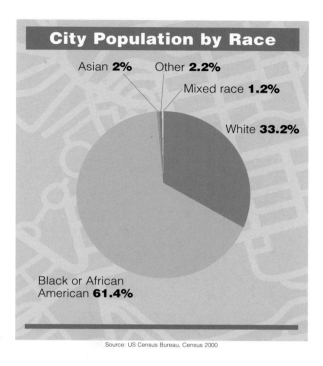

City Population by Race

Asian **2%**   Other **2.2%**
Mixed race **1.2%**
White **33.2%**
Black or African American **61.4%**

Source: US Census Bureau, Census 2000

Fifteenth Amendment to the Constitution passed in 1870 guarantees the right to vote regardless of race, color, or previous condition of servitude. Despite both this and the Civil Rights Act passed by the U.S. Congress in 1875 (which the Supreme Court declared unconstitutional in 1883), African Americans were excluded from voting and politics because of racial prejudice. "Jim Crow" laws limited the African Americans' civil rights and made segregation the law of the land. Unable to enter the white business world of Atlanta, African Americans created their own businesses, communities, and schools within the city.

Segregation and race riots separated the black and white communities even further; many African American Atlantans headed north where there were available jobs and no

Charlayne Hunter-Gault

Determined to follow in the footsteps of her childhood hero, Brenda Starr, the comic strip newswoman, Charlayne Hunter (pictured right with her husband Ronald Gault) decided to become a journalist. A resident of Atlanta, she found that the only journalism program in the state was at the University of Georgia, which, in 1959, was an all-white school. Supported by local civil rights activists, Charlayne Hunter and Hamilton Holmes, a high school friend, requested an integration order from the federal court in 1959. She attended Wayne State University until the court issued the integration order in 1961, when she and Hamilton Holmes became the first African American students to enter the University of Georgia, which became a huge media event.

Hunter-Gault graduated with her degree in journalism in 1963, then worked for New Yorker *magazine, the* New York Times *newspaper, and, in 1978, became the national correspondent for PBS's MacNeil/Lehrer NewsHour. Her experience of being the subject of a news story in 1961 helped form her insightful and respectful interviewing style. The recipient of many awards for her journalistic excellence, Hunter-Gault is a well-respected public speaker who has shed light on many difficult subjects, including issues of apartheid and racism. Today, she is bureau chief and news correspondent for CNN International in Johannesburg, South Africa.*

segregation laws. For those who remained, Auburn Avenue, just east of the downtown business district, became the center of Atlanta's African American business enterprises. Atlanta also had a good number of African American college graduates thanks to the four universities in the city— Atlanta University (established in 1865), Clark College (1869), Morehouse College (1867), and Spelman College (1881).

Equality Takes Hold

During the Great Depression, many more African Americans left Atlanta for the northern cities where they hoped to find jobs. The federal government's New Deal programs, which were begun to help people through the Depression, not only employed the remaining workers but created a new government bureaucracy in which Atlanta's college-educated African Americans were able to obtain positions as social workers, teachers, and program managers. The self-help groups that also arose in African American communities in response to the Depression became the basis for future businesses. These two trends began to create a strong African American middle class.

When World War II (1939–1945) came, African Americans were needed to support the war effort and moved into factory and other jobs previously held only by white workers. As they became an increasingly critical part of the Atlanta work force, their social activism and opposition to Jim Crow laws increased as well. The Atlanta Urban League became increasingly active in working for better schools, housing, and jobs for African Americans and also registered many to vote. Thus began the Civil Rights era, when African Americans all over the United States used politics and civil disobedience to establish new laws that insured their equality in the country.

Eventually, African Americans gained equality in both business and in government and social services in Atlanta. Since 1973, when Maynard Jackson was elected as the first black mayor of a large Southern city, African American mayors have guided Atlanta's growth to become a world-class

"I have a dream that one day this nation will rise up and live out the true meaning of its creed: We hold these truths to be self-evident: that all men are created equal."

—Martin Luther King Jr., in his speech at the Lincoln Memorial on August 28, 1963.

city. A new national trend began in the 1990s: African Americans began to move back to Atlanta from the northern cities.

New Arrivals

The newest people to move into Atlanta and become part of the city are Hispanic and Asian American. Many of the Asian Americans arrived as fairly recent refugees from their home countries. The Hispanic Americans, primarily from Mexico, arrived to work as farmworkers and laborers—many fleeing an economically depressed country where they could find no work. They and their families are now a part of Atlanta. In an interesting trend, Atlanta's new immigrants work in multi-ethnic areas instead of isolating themselves in individual ethnic communities.

Religion

The city of Atlanta contains nearly a thousand churches, synagogues, and other places of worship. The primary religion in the city is Protestant Christianity, and the African American Baptist churches have the greatest number of worshippers, approximately 30 percent of the churchgoing population.

African American Baptist churches grew out of the old tradition of "slave preachers," the African Americans who learned about the Christian religion and shared it with their fellow slaves, mixing messages from the Bible with the chanting, singing, hand-clapping participation of their African heritage. These preachers began to establish regular churches: The first African American Baptist church was begun near Savannah, Georgia, in 1775.

▼ *A commemorative service in honor of Martin Luther King Jr. is held annually at the Ebenezer Baptist Church in Atlanta's Sweet Auburn neighborhood.*

Since mixed-race worship is fairly recent in southern history, the African Americans created their own Baptist church structure, and, in 1895, the National Baptist Convention was formed, which is one of the largest religious organizations in the United States. Other African American denominations, such as the African Methodist Episcopal Church (AME) are popular in Atlanta, along with the United Methodist Church.

One famous church in Atlanta is the Ebenezer Baptist Church, where Martin Luther King Jr.'s father and grandfather were pastors and where King was a copastor

▲ *Each spring, Atlanta's Dogwood Festival offers a variety of entertainment centered on Piedmond Park.*

during the Civil Rights Movement. The scene of many Civil Rights conferences and events in the 1960s, this church is being restored as a national historic site. The New Birth Missionary Baptist Church is a newer mega-church, where the congregation numbers twenty-five thousand members. The large arena-like structure is used for services inspired by the African American religious tradition.

After its early beginnings, Judaism continued to grow in Atlanta, which has more than seventeen synagogues. In 1887, a group of fewer than twenty men founded the Ahavath Achim congregation in a small room in Atlanta. Today, their Buckhead-area synagogue serves seventeen hundred families, many of them fourth- and fifth-generation Atlantans, and is the Southeast's largest Conservative Jewish synagogue.

Festivals and Celebrations

This is the city of the annual Dogwood Festival, Atlanta's largest celebration. Since 1936, Atlantans have been gathering each April in Piedmont Park to celebrate the beauty of the native dogwood trees in bloom.

Coca-Cola's Humble Beginnings

In 1886, "Doc" Pemberton, an Atlanta patent medicine maker, created the formula for Coca-Cola in an iron pot in his backyard, called it the ideal brain tonic, and sold it as a medicine. Few people bought it so he sold his formula for $2,300 to another druggist, Asa Candler, who continued to mix the Coca-Cola syrup with tap water and sell it as a medicine. One day, however, a customer got his syrup mixed with soda water by accident. Soon, many people wanted a glass of the refreshing bubbly drink, so Candler began to sell it as a soda-fountain drink. Coca-Cola made Candler a millionaire and today, more than one billion drinks are consumed each day that are made by the Coca-Cola Company. The World of Coca-Cola Pavilion in downtown (pictured above) houses a huge collection of Coca-Cola memorabilia.

Garden club members and city boosters promoted early festivals, but during the 1990s, the festival, the largest cultural event in the Southeast, expanded to three different parks for eight days. Drawing more than 400,000 visitors, the Dogwood Festival includes varied events such as home tours, a parade, a hot-air balloon race, music, and arts and crafts displays.

Sponsored by the city, another big Atlanta festival is the annual Jazz Festival, held during May for twenty-seven years. Featuring local and international talent, this month of jazz programs finishes with three big days of music throughout Atlanta over the Memorial Day weekend, in the country's largest free jazz festival.

Christmas in Atlanta is not a scene of horse-drawn sleighs, children ice-skating, and families gathered around fireplaces as the snow falls. The climate is too warm for that. It is, however, celebrated with many events, beginning with the lighting of Rich's Great Tree in Underground Atlanta at Thanksgiving. The Atlanta Symphony Orchestra's musical series features traditional Christmas music throughout December, while Christmas at Callanwolde opens up the huge, festively decorated mansion, former home of the Coca-Cola founder's son, to the public. The Egleston Children's Christmas Parade, held in downtown Atlanta on the first Saturday of December, features balloons, floats, and Santa Claus. The Centennial Olympic Park and the Georgia World Congress Center across the street put on a Festival of Lights and a Festival of Trees for all to enjoy the beautiful twinkling lights, decorated trees, and a miniature train while they stroll around the park and convention center for the winter holidays of Chanukah and Christmas.

Food

Atlanta's diverse population is reflected in the choice of hundreds of restaurants available serving Chinese, Colombian, Cuban, Japanese, Thai, Mexican, and Indian foods. However, Atlantans also savor their Southern cooking, with such regional specialties as fried eggs, country ham, and grits for breakfast, a sliced barbecued pork sandwich for lunch, and dinner with fried chicken, catfish, or chicken-fried steak, black-eyed peas, collard greens, cornbread or biscuits, and for dessert, peach cobbler or sweet potato pie. Southern-style cooking combines typical American fare with African American specialties. Southerners pride themselves on the quality of their barbecue, which is meat cooked in a spicy sauce on a grill, and hominy grits (made from specially prepared dried corn) can be found everywhere, replacing bread and rice.

▼ *Miss Pittypat's Porch, a well-known downtown Atlanta restaurant, serves southern food, such as the meal of corn, shrimp, and potatoes pictured below, in a* Gone with the Wind *setting.*

CHAPTER 3

Living in Atlanta

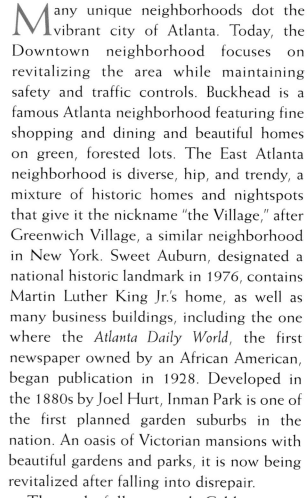

Many unique neighborhoods dot the vibrant city of Atlanta. Today, the Downtown neighborhood focuses on revitalizing the area while maintaining safety and traffic controls. Buckhead is a famous Atlanta neighborhood featuring fine shopping and dining and beautiful homes on green, forested lots. The East Atlanta neighborhood is diverse, hip, and trendy, a mixture of historic homes and nightspots that give it the nickname "the Village," after Greenwich Village, a similar neighborhood in New York. Sweet Auburn, designated a national historic landmark in 1976, contains Martin Luther King Jr.'s home, as well as many business buildings, including the one where the *Atlanta Daily World*, the first newspaper owned by an African American, began publication in 1928. Developed in the 1880s by Joel Hurt, Inman Park is one of the first planned garden suburbs in the nation. An oasis of Victorian mansions with beautiful gardens and parks, it is now being revitalized after falling into disrepair.

The colorfully named Cabbagetown originated as a workingman's neighborhood with houses built by the nearby Fulton Bag & Cotton Mill for the mill workers. After the mill closed, the Victorian row houses and

◀ *Spelman College, seen here, is part of the Atlanta University Center, the largest African American education center in the United States.*

shotgun cottages were offered to their occupants and became single-family homes. The neighborhood declined when the mills shut down, but artists, musicians, and young families are now purchasing and restoring the modest homes.

Housing

Many people have been moving to single-family homes in the suburban neighborhoods surrounding Atlanta. More than two-thirds of the people in metropolitan Atlanta own their own homes whether they are in a suburban development or a condominium in a downtown high-rise building.

Atlanta's low-income citizens are eligible for housing assistance through the Atlanta Housing Authority. Serving approximately fifty thousand people, the authority has pioneered the use of mixed-use and mixed-income developments that include low-income housing as one part of the neighborhood. Low-income residents select from a number of choices that include high-rise apartments in the center of the city or town houses in suburban communities with schools and shops. The award-winning Centennial Place features a community that includes low-income housing units, an elementary school, a bank, and a YMCA (Young Men's Christian Association).

Created at the turn of the century by urban planner Frederick Law Olmsted, founder of American landscape achitecture, one of the city's most magnificent neighborhoods is Druid Hills. It features lush

▼ *A tour guide describes Atlanta's attractive Druid Hills neighborhood. Long a tourist attraction, Druid Hills provided the location for the Academy Award-winning movie* Driving Miss Daisy.

Underground Atlanta

Historically, Atlanta grew up around the trains, whose tracks choked the city. Huge viaducts were built over the train tracks, and Atlanta's people and traffic moved up and over the rails. Underground Atlanta is a renovation of an original underground train complex located in the heart of Atlanta. It features six blocks, 12 acres (5 ha), and three levels of entertainment under the city streets. In an effort in 2004 to expand Underground Atlanta as the city's premier entertainment district, new restaurants and nightclubs joined the existing shops and activities. As many as 350,000 Atlantans gather here on New Year's Eve to watch the giant peach fall from the Underground's 138-foot (42-m) light tower, heralding the New Year. The underground complex is reached by steps (pictured right) leading from a busy piazza.

parks, tree-lined boulevards, and heavily forested green spaces and lots. Many Atlanta developers involved in the creation of Druid Hills went on to incorporate Olmsted's concepts in other developments, giving Atlanta its reputation as a "garden city."

Markets and Malls

Some historic neighborhoods feature unique stores in renovated homes and storefronts along commercial streets. Ten miles (16 km) south of the city stands the State Farmer's Market, the largest open-air market in the eastern United States, which sells fresh fruit and vegetables, flowers, meats, and eggs.

Many people like to shop in malls, which gather a large variety of stores into a single, air-conditioned building. Hot and humid Atlanta has its share of shopping malls, including some beautiful, expensive ones in the Buckhead area that offer antique stores and other exclusive shops. The Mall of Georgia, opened in 1999 just north of Atlanta, featuring several department stores, is the largest mall in the southeastern United States. More than a dozen different malls circle downtown Atlanta.

Attractive Architecture

Atlanta native and architect John Portman influenced the design of this people-friendly city. He built the Hyatt Regency Atlanta in 1967 with a twenty-two-floor tall central atrium space, which large hotels worldwide have copied. He also designed Peachtree Center, which offers numerous clothing, furniture, accessories, music, and electronics stores combined with a diverse number of eateries and hotels. This gigantic complex of hotels, businesses, shopping, and entertainment contains individual buildings with central atriums connected with aboveground walkways so that people can move from place to place without encountering street traffic. Rarely has a city been shaped so completely by the ideas of a single architect.

Blending with the big-business look of downtown Atlanta are bits and pieces of the old Atlanta, carefully preserved. Built in 1897, the city's oldest high-rise, known as the Flatiron Building, and the Candler Building, a seventeen-story triangular structure built in 1906, stand next to modern skyscrapers.

Education

Metropolitan Atlanta has 700 public schools serving about 500,000 students. The public-school systems include Fulton, DeKalb, and Cobb County school systems as well as other county school systems, the city school system, and 185 private and church-supported schools. Most children attend public school and graduate from high school; public schooling is free for the families as it is paid for with local taxes.

Atlanta Public Schools, the city's kindergarten through grade twelve public-school system, was established in 1869, and its first school opened three years later. Today, there are eighty-nine schools in the system serving fifty-four thousand students. An elected, nine-member board of education administers the sixty-three elementary

▼ As part of a campaign to promote exercise and nutrition, Carla McGhee of the Women's National Basketball Association is seen here showing children at an Atlanta elementary school how to do push-ups.

Atlanta University Center

The Atlanta University Center is the largest group of historically black colleges in the country and includes Clark Atlanta University (formed when Atlanta University and Clark College merged in 1988), the Interdenominational Theological Center, the Morehouse School of Medicine, and Morehouse, Morris Brown, and Spelman Colleges. Beginning in 1865 with the founding of Atlanta University, this group of colleges offered—and still offers—the opportunity of higher education to African Americans and played an important role in the Civil Rights Movement in Atlanta. Martin Luther King Jr. graduated from Morehouse College, and the Morehouse and Spelman students organized sit-ins, boycotts, and marches in Atlanta beginning in 1960.

schools (kindergarten through fifth grade), sixteen middle schools (grades sixth through ninth) and ten high schools (grades tenth through twelfth) in the Atlanta Public Schools.

Atlanta is home to more than fifteen institutions of higher education, both public and private, including the noted Georgia Institute of Technology (Georgia Tech) and Emory University. One of Atlanta's top research universities, Georgia Tech is always ranked one of the top ten public universities in the United States and produces some of the nation's top engineers and scientists.

The Methodist church founded Emory University, located in Atlanta's Druid Hills, in 1836. One of the nation's foremost private universities, Emory has received major donations throughout the years from various Coca-Cola executives. Known for its high academic standards and emphasis on ethics, Emory's theology program and medical, business, and law schools rank among the nation's finest; Emory University itself is one of the top twenty-five universities in the country.

Trains, Cars, and Rapid Transit

From its historic beginnings, Atlanta has been a transportation hub. The railroads made Atlanta, and the city continued to be a huge railway center both before and after the Civil War. The large, elegant Terminal Station opened in 1905 and served millions of travelers, becoming an Atlanta landmark until its closure in 1970 and demolition in 1972. A well-known saying after the Civil War was "Whether you're heading for paradise or hell, you have to change trains in Atlanta." In the 1920s, the railroads were the largest employers in Atlanta, spending millions of dollars and providing over twenty thousand jobs. The railroad tracks also carved the city into neighborhoods and defined boundaries within the city.

Soon horses and railroads gave way to automobiles and streetcars, especially for inner-city transportation. During the 1950s and 1960s, Atlanta grew, as did its roads. Today, the Interstate 285 beltway surrounds

Atlanta in a large loop, with other freeways crisscrossing Atlanta like spokes on a wheel. Everything inside the loop, or "the Perimeter" as it is called, is considered to be part of Atlanta. Downtown, Peachtree Street is the main north-south road and a symbol of the city. In spite of the freeway system, traffic is a problem in Atlanta and adds to the pollution of the city.

In the 1960s, the need for a modern rapid-transit system was evident, and the Metropolitan Atlanta Rapid Transit Authority, or MARTA, was born. In the beginning, MARTA purchased and upgraded the Atlanta Transit System (ATS), the city bus system. In the 1970s, long-range planning added the rapid rail system to the existing bus system, and one of the best rapid transit systems in a large metropolitan area was built. Today, MARTA focuses on maintaining and expanding its popular rail system while increasing security. MARTA's services helped Atlanta win the competition to be the site of the 1996 Olympics.

Hartsfield-Jackson Atlanta International Airport competes with Chicago's O'Hare International for the title of the world's busiest airport. It boasts the largest passenger terminal complex in the world with 5.7 million square feet (529,500 square meters) and 146 domestic and 28 international gates. Over 79 million passengers used the airport in 2003, proving that Atlanta continues its role as a transportation center in the twenty-first century. It also serves as a headquarters and hub for Delta Airlines.

MARTA

For $1.75, anyone can ride MARTA to anywhere in the city of Atlanta or Fulton and DeKalb Counties. The ninth largest such system in North America, MARTA has more than forty-five hundred employees, thirty-eight rail stations, and 48 miles (77 km) of rail. Operating 691 buses, 110 vans for the disabled, and 350 rail cars, MARTA serves an average of a half million passengers each day. During the seventeen days of the 1996 Centennial Olympic Games in Atlanta, more than 25 million passengers (1.5 million passengers a day) rode MARTA.

CHAPTER 4

Atlanta at Work

In 2000, the U.S. stock market began a downturn that affected business earnings and economies across the nation; the terrorist attacks on September 11, 2001, further affected business, especially the travel, hotel, tourist, and convention businesses. Atlanta's economy is recovering from both these events. Luckily, its economy is as diverse as its people, so Atlanta has not suffered as much as other major cities.

In its March 2004 issue, *Inc.* magazine named Atlanta number one of its "Top 25 Cities for Doing Business in America."

The Cable News Network

Ted Turner started his media empire in 1970 when he purchased a failing Atlanta UHF channel and turned it into the beginning of the TBS (Turner Broadcasting System) empire. Ten years later, he used profits from this enterprise to start CNN, the only twenty-four-hour news channel on cable television. Located downtown at One CNN Center, CNN and TBS occupy a former shopping mall across from the Centennial Olympic Park. The four buildings sharing an atrium were renovated in 1999. Now a major tourist attraction, the CNN Studio Tour allows visitors to see behind the scenes of an international, nonstop news organization. CNN has made major contributions to the revitalization of Atlanta's downtown area. The picture (left) shows the CNN media team at work.

Calling the large city affordable, with a diverse economy and such assets as excellent colleges and universities and a world-class airport, the article also promoted Atlanta's quality of life and central city.

Major Employers

A wide variety of businesses make their homes in Atlanta—transportation, banking, communications, insurance, retail, and technology firms as well as government employers and small businesses. Reflecting the city's strengths, the Metro Atlanta Chamber of Commerce is currently seeking new businesses in the following areas: corporate headquarters, biosciences, logistics/transportation, telecommunications, and computer software.

Atlanta owes a lot to its position as a transportation and communications hub, which forms the backbone of the city's economic life. Top employers in these categories include BellSouth, AT&T, Cox Communications, Cingular Wireless, and Delta Airlines and United Parcel Service, (both of which have their headquarters in Atlanta).

Atlanta's low cost of living, good quality of life, international transportation links, and access to an educated population have lured many major corporations to make their headquarters in Atlanta. In addition to professional and business services such as insurance companies, banks, and computing companies, major corporations with

"'Hotlanta' is precisely that, the hottest of the hot economies of the country."

—Joel Kotkin, *Inc.* magazine, March 2004.

headquarters here include Home Depot, Georgia-Pacific, and SunTrust Banks. Coca-Cola and CNN (Cable News Network) are longtime Atlanta residents and have been joined by Chick-fil-A and Holiday Inn, among others. Atlanta is presently home to thirteen Fortune 500 company headquarters, the five hundred U.S.-based corporations with the largest revenues in the country.

Government and education represent the other major employers in Atlanta. Emory University, Gwinnett County schools, Cobb County schools, the U.S. Postal Service, and the U.S. Center for Disease Control are some of the places where Atlantans work. In addition, Atlanta is large enough to attract a number of business conventions and tourists, which contribute to the hospitality and service economy of the city.

Home Depot, the largest company headquartered in Atlanta, began doing business right there in 1978 and today is the world's largest home-improvement retailer, with fifteen hundred stores in North America. Their stores stock 35,000 building, lawn, and garden items and employ more than 300,000 people.

Founded in 1886 in Atlanta, the Coca-Cola Company produces over four hundred soft-drink brands for markets worldwide.

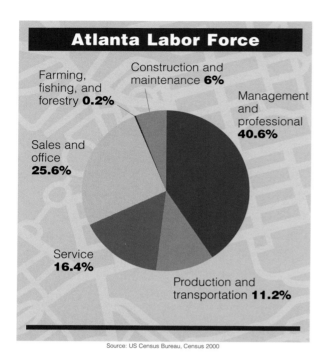

Atlanta Labor Force

Farming, fishing, and forestry **0.2%**

Construction and maintenance **6%**

Management and professional **40.6%**

Sales and office **25.6%**

Service **16.4%**

Production and transportation **11.2%**

Source: US Census Bureau, Census 2000

With more than six billion customers in two hundred countries, Coca-Cola remains the brand that most people around the world associate with the United States, and so, of all the businesses headquartered in Atlanta, it is probably the city's most famous.

Running the City

Atlanta has a mayor-council form of government. The mayor, city council president, and eighteen members of the city council are all elected for four-year terms. Each city council member represents a different district of the city of Atlanta. In 2001, Mayor Shirley Franklin was elected the fifty-eighth mayor of Atlanta in a landslide victory and began serving in January 2002 as the city's first woman mayor and the first African American

woman elected to lead a major Southern city. The city's seventy-two hundred employees report to her through her chief operating officer.

In addition, the city of Atlanta lies within two different Georgia counties, which also have governing responsibility for the area. Atlanta's city government sometimes shares responsibility with Fulton County for certain departments, such as the city/county library system. Atlanta is home to more than sixty other local governing bodies, including various county governments, local boards of education, and a regional transit authority. Atlanta works cooperatively with them all, especially Fulton and DeKalb Counties, where most of Atlanta lies. The Georgia court system is likewise a checkerboard of municipal, county, state and federal courts, similar to most other states in the United States.

Inside City Government

Atlanta's city government provides police, fire, parks, recreation, water, wastewater, planning, development, traffic, and street services. Current city programs focus on trash cleanup and removal and pothole repairs in the streets. Recent new or revitalized projects led by the mayor's office include the Living Wage Commission, an Ethics Commission to insure that city government is open and honest, and "Let's Do Downtown," a program to bring people downtown for various events and entertainments.

Maynard Jackson

Maynard Jackson (pictured above) served three terms as Atlanta's first African American mayor from 1974 to 1982 and again from 1990 to 1994. A child prodigy, Jackson began studying at Morehouse University in Atlanta at age fourteen and graduated at eighteen. He went on to become a lawyer, noted for his excellent public speaking skills. While mayor, he began a unique affirmative-action program that engaged many minority-owned businesses to build city projects. His accomplishments during his first two terms established Atlanta's identity as a city of growth and opportunity for all.

Atlanta has additional nongovernmental boards, commissions, and agencies that cooperatively help govern the city. The Atlanta Housing Authority and Atlanta Development Authority work to make sure that the city residents have safe, affordable homes and that funding is provided to encourage growth and development in previously rundown areas of the city. A mix of taxes and fees, including property tax, sales tax, and various fees for permits and business licenses, helps to pay for the city's public services.

Issues and Problems

Atlanta suffers from many of the same problems that plague other large cities. Budget deficits, poverty, homelessness, crime, drug use, and substandard housing all contribute to the decay of this vibrant city. City residents are dissatisfied with city services—garbage and litter are not picked up promptly and streets are not repaired in a timely manner.

The current administration is addressing some problems. For example, the Commission on Homelessness created a "Blueprint to End Homelessness in Atlanta in Ten Years" in 2003. From this

"We stand not so much as a gateway to the South, but as a gateway to a new time, a new era, a new beginning for the cities of our land."

—Maynard Jackson, January 1974 inaugural address.

33

comprehensive plan, the city has selected seven recommendations to put into action immediately.

Atlanta cannot pay for the services it does provide; it is also struggling to eliminate an $82 million budget deficit through many cuts in city departments, including a cut to the mayor's salary. At the

▲ *The Atlanta City Hall pictured here opened in 1930 and housed the city government offices until 1989, when they moved to the City Hall Annex nearby. This historic City Hall is still used for City Council meetings.*

same time, Atlanta is hiring more police officers to make the city a safer place. As Atlanta grows and becomes a more popular place to live, the cost of living there increases, and some residents worry that they won't be able to afford to live in the city any more.

One problem that has eclipsed all others is the crumbling of the Atlanta's aging sewer system, which has made international news and embarrassed the city. Due to Atlanta's enormous growth, 250 million gallons (950 million liters) of treated sewage go into the river daily, and during rainstorms, millions of gallons of untreated sewage spill into the river when the treatment plant can't handle the overflow. In 1999, Atlanta was fined $2.5 million for violations of the federal Clean Water Act and forced to improve water quality in the Chattahoochee River, which is rated as one of the five most polluted waterways in the United States where it passes through Atlanta.

This problem has been ignored for a long time, until the price tag to fix the city's sewage treatment plant and sewer system has risen to $3 billion. Mayor Shirley Franklin is addressing the problem with a combination of increased sewer fees, a sales tax increase dedicated strictly to fixing the sewers, and state and federal dollars. Franklin's Clean Water Atlanta program was also put in place to educate the public about how they can help, to improve existing water treatment plants, and to build combined sewer-overflow underground tunnels that will take water to a new water-treatment plant.

THE CARTER CENTER

Jimmy Carter

A native of Plains, Georgia, Jimmy Carter (pictured above) moved from Atlanta's Governor's Mansion to the White House. One-time Georgia governor (1971–1975), Carter served as the thirty-ninth president of the United States from 1977 to 1981. Known for initiating the Camp David Peace Accords between Egypt and Israel, Carter continues to be an advocate for peace, human rights, and social justice. He began the Carter Center in Atlanta (see page 43) in 1982, a private organization that partners with others to sponsor worldwide programs that promote peace and health and eliminate hunger. In 1984, he joined Habitat for Humanity, an organization that helps people to build their own homes; he continues to work building houses and in other capacities. In 2002, Jimmy Carter was awarded the Nobel Peace Prize.

CHAPTER 5

Atlanta at Play

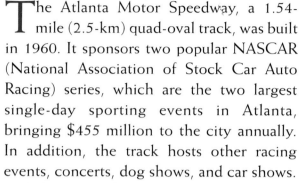

The Atlanta Motor Speedway, a 1.54-mile (2.5-km) quad-oval track, was built in 1960. It sponsors two popular NASCAR (National Association of Stock Car Auto Racing) series, which are the two largest single-day sporting events in Atlanta, bringing $455 million to the city annually. In addition, the track hosts other racing events, concerts, dog shows, and car shows.

Atlanta is home to several major professional sports teams, including the Atlanta Braves baseball team. The Braves gave the city its first national championship when they won the World Series in 1995. Turner Field, which opened in 1997, is currently the "Home of the Braves" and a major Atlanta landmark. This state-of-the-art playing field features the latest in technology, including more than five hundred television monitors. Turner Field also has a park area called Monument Grove that honors baseball's greats. Hank Aaron, who still makes his home in Atlanta, is noted for hitting 755 home runs in his major league career, and a photograph 100 feet (30 m) in diameter of his last home run dominates the Grand Entry Plaza at Turner Field.

The Atlanta Falcons, a National Football League (NFL) team, have called that city home since 1965. They originally

◀ *Atlanta's annual three-day Music Midtown Festival draws hundreds of thousands of fans to the city.*

Peach Bowl

Atlanta's bowl game, the Chick-fil-A Peach Bowl, is the most competitive college football post-season bowl game. Held each year in the Georgia Dome, the 2004 game was the seventh sold-out game in a row; attendance was nearly 72,000. The payout to the teams and their colleges was $2.2 million, the highest ever. The prestigious Bobby Dodd Coach of the Year Award is announced at halftime. The Peach Bowl has given over a million dollars to local charities and hosts a game-day parade with more than one hundred entries. The picture (above) shows the University of Maryland Terrapins playing the University of Tennessee Volunteers in the 2003 game.

shared the Atlanta-Fulton County Stadium with the Atlanta Braves, but in 1992, the Georgia Dome was built on the western side of downtown for the team. In 1994 and 2000, the Super Bowl, professional football's most important game, was played at the Georgia Dome.

Philips Arena, close by the Georgia Dome, opened in 1999 as the home for two professional sports teams—the Atlanta Hawks basketball team and the Atlanta Thrashers hockey team. The $213-million arena also serves as a major concert venue for Atlanta. Owned by local business multimillionaire Ted Turner, both teams and the arena were sold to a local coalition, Atlanta Spirit LLC, in 2004.

▲ *The elegant Swan House in Buckhead forms a major part of the Atlanta History Center.*

From Hip-Hop to Classical

Atlanta has a vibrant music scene that is well known for its hip-hop and rhythm-and-blues artists, although country, pop, rock, jazz and gospel also flourish. Those who call Atlanta home include Whitney Houston, Elton John, Jermaine Dupri, REM, Faith Evans, Outkast, Ludacris, Dottie Peoples, Black Crowes, TLC, Travis Tritt, Usher, and the Indigo Girls. In 2004, the eleventh annual Music Midtown Festival on 40 acres (16 ha) featured over ninety different bands in three days. Clubs and bars highlight the local music scene, especially the southern hip-hop for which Atlanta is famous.

Atlanta is also home to the Atlanta Symphony Orchestra, which was started in 1945 by some local youth musicians. Now ninety-five members strong, it plays more than two hundred concerts each year to audiences that top half a million annually.

A Sense of History

Those looking for the gracious old South in today's Atlanta can enjoy various historical locations. Although the city of Atlanta has never been the location of any of the South's large plantation homes, there are some beautiful mansions available for tourists to view—in spite of Atlanta's historic fires. The author of *Gone with the Wind* lived in an apartment at 999 Peachtree Street when she wrote her book. Margaret Mitchell called her apartment "The Dump," but today the whole house is a museum featuring her life and work. Visitors can also tour the home of Joel Chandler Harris, author of the Uncle Remus tales, who called his charming 1870 Queen Anne-style home the "Wren's Nest."

The Atlanta History Center purchased the Swan House, built in 1928, and the ten surrounding acres (4 ha) to create a display of nineteenth-century Georgia farm buildings and featuring a typical early plantation home, the Tullie Smith House, built by Robert Smith. The house was built in 1845 and inhabited until 1967. It includes a blacksmith shop, a barn, and a separate kitchen. McElreath Hall Library and Archives, finished in 1975, houses the History Center's collection of 3.5 million prints, photographs, books, drawings, postcards, scrapbooks, and maps featuring historic Atlanta.

Theater and the Arts

Ranking with the New York's Lincoln Center for the Performing Arts, Washington, D.C.'s John F. Kennedy Center for the Performing Arts, and Los Angeles Music Center, the Woodruff Arts Center is the creative hub of the city. The center is made up of the Alliance Theater, the Atlanta College of Art, the Atlanta Symphony Orchestra, the High

Museum of Art, and the Fourteenth Street Playhouse. Begun in 1968 to commemorate 106 Atlanta arts supporters who died in a 1962 Paris plane crash, the Atlanta Memorial Arts Center later combined with the High Museum of Art to become the Robert A. Woodruff Arts Center in 1985.

▼ *Built in the 1920s and rescued from destruction in the 1970s, the Fox Theater on Peachtree Street is today an arts center and a historic Atlanta landmark.*

The Woodruff Center campus in midtown Atlanta consists of seven buildings housing a symphony hall, art museum, five live theater stages, two art galleries, an arts library, sculpture garden, box office, and work space for more than 550 musicians, artists, curators, and professors. A planned expansion features a new Atlanta College of Art designed by Renzo Piano as well as a complete renovation of the High Museum of Art, which will weave the art facilities into the surrounding neighborhood. The Atlanta Symphony Orchestra will also be getting a new building designed by Santiago Calatrava, a well-known Spanish architect, scheduled for completion in 2008.

1996 Summer Olympics

Atlanta was chosen as the site of the 1996 Centennial Olympic Games; the city rose to the occasion, working feverishly to provide world-class sports venues. Heavyweight boxing champion Muhammad Ali, who won a gold medal at the 1960 Olympics in Rome, accepted the Olympic torch after its 15,000-mile (24,000-km) journey across the United States and lit the Olympic flame on the opening day on July 19, 1996, in Atlanta's Olympic Stadium. A record 10,318 athletes from 197 different countries participated in 271 events; 28 countries competed in the Olympics for the first time ever. On July 27, 1996, the Centennial Olympic Park bombing took place, killing one person and wounding 111 others. The games continued, however, and after a long search, the bomber, Eric Robert Rudolph, was finally arrested in 2003. He has also been charged with bombing a women's health center and a nightclub.

Parks and Plants

The city of Atlanta maintains more than one hundred city parks; in addition, there are many county and other park facilities in the Atlanta metropolitan area. Grant Park in Atlanta is one of the original city parks. It houses the Cyclorama, which is an enormous circular painting of the Civil War battle that resulted in the fall of Atlanta on July 22, 1864. Visitors stand on a viewing platform, and the painting revolves around them. Twelve Polish, Austrian, and German artists painted the cyclorama from 1885 to 1886. Grant Park is also home to Zoo Atlanta, the city's zoo.

Centennial Olympic Park, the city's legacy and monument to the 1996 Olympics, was built as an area where people could gather together. With 750 trees, 50,000 shrubs, 330,000 square feet (30,660 sq m) of grass, statues, and art, this beautiful space is truly a gift to Atlanta residents and visitors. The centerpiece, an 82.5-foot- (25-m-) long fountain of rings featuring 251 water jets, is a lasting memorial to the Olympic Games.

In 1976, the Atlanta Botanical Garden was started in order to collect and display plants. The garden contains more than 15 acres (6 ha) of planted areas for people to

Stone Mountain

Stone Mountain (pictured left) is the main feature of Stone Mountain Park, located just outside Atlanta. The world's largest high-relief sculpture is carved into the side of the granite, 825-feet- (250-m-) tall mountain. The sculpture portrays three of the South's Civil War heroes— General Thomas "Stonewall" Jackson, General Robert E. Lee, and Confederate president Jefferson Davis. The carving is 90 feet (27 m) high and 190 feet (58 m) long and towers 400 feet (122 m) above the base of the mountain. Workers could stand inside the curve of a horse's ear or in the horse's mouth to escape a rain shower. Although Mrs. C. Helen Plane had the idea for this sculpture in 1909, it was not completed until 1972, after three different sculptors worked on it.

wander in and enjoy, as well as endangered plants from rainforests and deserts raised here in conservatories. Well known for its collections of orchids, conifers, and carnivorous plants, the Atlanta Botanical Garden is proud of its conservation programs, especially those that seek to restore the endangered native plant communities in boggy areas of the southeastern United States. Storza Woods, also a part of the Botanical Garden, is an inner-city hardwood forest that allows visitors to wander through and imagine what Atlanta used to look like when the Creek Indians lived there.

Vacation Destinations

The top vacation destination for Atlantans is Lake Lanier. Located just thirty minutes north of Atlanta on the Chattahoochee River, the lake welcomes families with its water park, beach, fishing, boating, golf course, horse stables, and campgrounds.

Stone Mountain Park is most famous for its sculpture, but the surrounding park area also provides entertainment to Atlantans and visitors. It features camping and hiking, a museum, waterslides, a plantation and farmyard experience for children, a scenic railroad, and a laser show that uses the side of the famous mountain as a screen.

CHAPTER 6

Looking Forward

The city, which recently had a budget shortfall, is tightening its belt, and, at the same time, spending what is necessary to attract further business to Atlanta. The brand new Georgia International Convention Center opened in 2003 right next door to Hartsfield-Jackson Atlanta International Airport, and the downtown Georgia World Congress Center completed a major expansion in 2002, getting ready for all of the conferences and conventions that will be coming Georgia's way in the future.

Atlanta also has several exciting development projects in progress. The Georgia Aquarium, a planned attraction that will contain 5 million gallons (19 million l) of saltwater and freshwater and more than fifty thousand aquatic animals, is scheduled to open in 2005 along with a remodeled World of Coca-Cola. Atlantic Station, which is being called the largest planned mixed development in the country, uses a 138-acre (56-ha) former steel mill site in midtown Atlanta. Developers have cleaned the site and built houses, townhouses, lofts, stores, apartments, shops, and parks for the residents. The Woodruff Arts Center development will also soon be completed.

Based in attractive parkland that overlooks downtown Atlanta, the Carter Center works in partnership with Emory University to promote peace, advance human rights, and alleviate suffering around the world.

Other Improvements

City transit may be improved with two proposed projects. One is a station where different types of transportation (such as bus and rail) would come together and use the same building. Another project, the Belt Line Transit Loop, would use existing abandoned railroad tracks to expand light-rail transportation to Atlanta's outlying areas.

Honoring and preserving its unique history, Atlanta just opened the King-Carter Freedom Peace Walk in 2003. This 1.5-mile (2.4-km) path with exhibits links the Carter Center, a nonprofit organization that promotes world peace and health projects, and the Martin Luther King Jr. National Historic Site. These two Nobel Prize winners' organizations will continue to inspire everyone to work for peace and freedom everywhere.

The current mayor hopes to make Atlanta not only a safe city but a caring one. Shirley Franklin sees a future Atlanta with an enhanced quality of life, a "city not just livable, but lovable."

"So, when I raise my gaze and look at the future of Atlanta, here's what I see. I see a city that is safe and clean. I see a city that cares for people, its own residents and visitors alike. I see a city governed honestly, openly and responsively."

—Mayor Shirley Franklin, January 5, 2004.

Carter Center

The Carter Center, founded in 1982 by former president Jimmy Carter and his wife, Rosalynn, promotes peace and fights disease in countries that are often forgotten in Asia, Africa, and South America.

In partnership with Emory University in Atlanta, the center has helped people in more than sixty-five different countries. It has observed elections in twenty-three countries, doubled grain outputs in fifteen African countries, and has reduced cases of Guinea worm disease from 3.5 million to less than 50,000 worldwide. Guinea worm disease is a parasitic worm infection caused by drinking contaminated water that affects poor communities, mainly in Africa.

In a June 2003 interview, Jimmy Carter says that his vision for the Carter Center has changed for the twenty-first century. When he began the center in 1982, he thought that its most important work would be to promote peace throughout the world. Now, he says, the gap between the rich and poor people in the world is growing, and poor people are more aware of this because of improved communications. He now thinks the most important job of the Carter Center is to help improve the lives of the world's poor by stamping out diseases and improving food supplies.

The Carter Center is located close to downtown Atlanta together with the Jimmy Carter Library and Museum.

Time Line

800–1500 The Native American Mound Builders flourish in northern Georgia and the Mississippi area, leaving large cities behind; they were gone by the time the Spanish explored Georgia in the 1540s.

1500s Native Americans including the Cherokee and the Creek live in the area of today's Atlanta.

1733 British Parliament grants charter for a new American colony, Georgia.

1749 Georgia's law against slavery is repealed.

1830s U.S. government forces Cherokee, Creek, and other tribes off their land.

1837 Western & Atlantic Railroad extends to Georgia and establishes its endpoint at Terminus.

1843 Terminus becomes Marthasville.

1845 Marthasville is renamed Atlanta.

1861 Georgia secedes from the United States; joins the Confederate States of America in the Civil War.

1864 General William T. Sherman burns down almost the entire city of Atlanta.

1865 Atlanta University opens its doors to educate African American students.

1868 Atlanta becomes Georgia's capital.

1869 Atlanta's public school system is established.

1880 Atlanta becomes Georgia's largest city.

1881 Atlanta hosts the first International Cotton Exposition.

1886 J. S. Pemberton creates Coca-Cola.

1889 The Georgia Capitol Building is completed in Atlanta.

1906 Atlanta's first and only race riot occurs.

1917 Atlanta burns again.

1936 Margaret Mitchell's *Gone with the Wind* is published and becomes an instant bestseller; the first federally funded low-income housing project is built in Atlanta.

1939 *Gone with the Wind* movie premieres in Atlanta.

1957 Martin Luther King Jr. and other Civil Rights activists start the Southern Christian Leadership Conference in Atlanta.

1965 Atlanta gets a National Football League (NFL) team, the Falcons.

1971 Jimmy Carter is elected Georgia's 76th governor.

1973 Maynard Jackson is elected Atlanta's first African American mayor.

1977 Jimmy Carter is inaugurated as president of the United States.

1980 Ted Turner starts Cable News Network (CNN).

1995 Atlanta Braves win the World Series.

1996 Centennial Summer Olympic Games held in Atlanta.

2001 Mayor Shirley Franklin is elected as Atlanta's first female mayor.

2002 Jimmy Carter is awarded the Nobel Peace Prize.

2004 *Inc.* magazine names Atlanta number one in its article "Top 25 Cities for Doing Business in the United States."

Glossary

activism taking direct action to achieve a political goal.

apartheid an official policy of racial segregation that used to be practiced by the Republic of South Africa.

atrium a many-storied central court in a building, usually topped with a skylight.

bureaucracy a system of organizational departments and their officials.

charter a written agreement that creates and defines the privileges of an organization.

civil disobedience refusing to obey laws in an effort to bring changes in government policies or legislation, usually using nonviolent means.

commemorate to honor the memory of someone or some event.

conservatories greenhouses for growing or displaying plants.

counterpart one thing similar to another.

demolition destruction of a building by explosives or wrecking ball.

diverse differing from one another.

exposition a public exhibit or show.

Great Depression the period of financial hardship from 1929 to 1939, when people lost their jobs, homes, farms, and businesses.

integration the act of making something open to people of all races.

patent medicine a packaged nonprescription drug; only the person or company making it knows its ingredients.

pedestrian designed for walking; also, a person on foot.

persecution injury or harassment on the basis of a difference in religion, country of origin, skin color, or other factor.

prodigy a person with exceptional talents or powers.

rapid transit fast passenger transportation in cities; for example, subways.

revitalized to make new again; to give new life.

segregation the separation of blacks and whites in transportation, restaurants, schools, and other aspects of public life.

shotgun cottage a house with several rooms joined in a straight line from front to back; in theory, one could shoot a shotgun in the front door and the pellet would exit the backdoor without hitting a wall.

venue a place where special events are held.

viaducts long, elevated roads, usually made of short spans supported by arches.

Further Information

Books

Berry, Carrie. *A Confederate Girl: The Diary of Carrie Berry*, 1864. Blue Earth Books, 2000.

Copolla, Jill, and Susan B. Gall. *Junior Worldmark Encyclopedia of World Cities: Atlanta, Georgia, to Denver, Colorado.* Gale Group, 2000.

Foulk, Karen. *147 Fun Things to Do in Atlanta.* Into Fun Company Publications, 2001.

Kent, Deborah. *Atlanta (Cities of the World).* Children's Press, 2001.

Knorr, Rosanne. *Kidding Around Atlanta.* Avalon Travel Publishing, 1997.

Marsh, Carole. *Meet Shirley Franklin, The Mayor of Atlanta.* Gallopade International, 2002.

Savage, Jeff. *Georgia (States).* Enslow Publishers, 2003.

Stechschulte, Pattie. *Georgia (From Sea to Shining Sea).* Scholastic Library Publishing, 2001.

Web Sites

www.atlantaga.gov
Explore the official Web site of the city of Atlanta, Georgia.

www.atlanta.georgia.gov
Find out more about the city of Atlanta and its attractions on this state government site.

www.ngeorgia.com/history/findex.html
Learn more about Native American history in northern Georgia.

www.ourgeorgiahistory.com
See an overview of Georgia's history as well as a time line.

www.stonemountainpark.com/newsite/education_cc_hist.asp
Find out more about the history of the Confederate carving at Stone Mountain.

Index